CW00468446

PITCAIR

AND

VACATION GUIDE

2024

Your trip

companion to

unwind and explore

Martha P. Rose

TABLE OF CONTENT

CHAPTER ONE

OVERVIEW OF PITCAIRN
ISLAND

Tucked away in the immensity
of the Pacific, Pitcairn Island is a
monument of tenacity, culture,
and seclusion. This small,
isolated island in the Pitcairn
Islands group has a turbulent

history that is linked to the historic Bounty mutiny. We uncover the facets of Pitcairn's distinct past, face its difficulties, and wonder at the island's timeless beauties that entice the daring traveller as we set out on a journey to discover it.

A. PITCAIRN ISLAND OVERVIEW

- **1. Locational coordinates:** Situated at roughly 25.07° S latitude and 130.10° W longitude, Pitcairn Island is one of the four islands that make up the Pitcairn Islands group. It is located more than 3,000 miles (4,800 km) east of New Zealand and is well known for being among the most isolated places on Earth with people. Its remoteness adds to a unique environment and an unmatched sense of seclusion.

- **2. Adjacent Waters:** The island's distinctive flora and wildlife have been sculpted by the unending expanse of the Pacific Ocean surrounding it. In addition to providing food for the locals, Pitcairn's glistening seas are a diver's gold mine, opening up a world of colourful marine life and breathtaking underwater scenery.

- **3. Weather and Climate:**Pitcairn enjoys year-round moderate temperatures due to its subtropical environment. El Niño occurrences can affect the weather patterns of the island, which is exposed to trade winds. The weather has a significant influence on living on Pitcairn and is partly responsible for the island's diverse topography and abundance of vegetation.

B. HISTORICAL IMPORTANCE

- **1. Settlement and Bounty Mutiny:**The history of Pitcairn is inextricably linked to that of the HMS Bounty, a British naval vessel most famous for the terrible mutiny that took place in 1789. A crew of mutineers led by Fletcher Christian took over the ship, abandoning Captain William Bligh. Together with their Tahitian allies, the mutineers found and made their home on Pitcairn Island while fleeing the British Navy. The remains of the Bounty, which the mutineers scuttled in order to avoid being discovered, may still be seen underwater and serve as a moving reminder of the turbulent past of the island. The Pitcairn Islanders, descended from the Bounty mutineers, are still residing on the island and are leaving a living legacy of this momentous occasion.

- **2. Pitcairn in the Present:** Lineage and Traditions about fifty people live on Pitcairn, most of whom being

4

descended from the original mutineers and their Tahitian companions. This little community has managed to preserve a unique culture that is a reflection of its maritime past and the fusion of European and Polynesian influences. Pitcairn Islanders feel a sense of continuity with their nautical ancestors because of their distinctive way of life, customs, and language, which provide a rare glimpse into a bygone past.

- **3. Historical Site Preservation:**Pitcairn's historical sites are of great importance to the islanders as well as to the world's historical legacy, which is why efforts are being made to conserve them. Inviting visitors to engage with the island's rich history are the Bounty's anchor, the mutineers' landing spot, and the graves of Fletcher Christian and other mutineers, all of which are kept in immaculate condition.

C. PARTICULAR DIFFICULTIES AND CHARMS

- **1. Distancing and Availability:**Pitcairn is incredibly isolated, which is both a draw and a difficulty. The island's isolation contributes to its pristine vistas but also presents logistical difficulties for visitors. Accessing Pitcairn is an experience in and of itself due to the limited alternatives for transportation, which include periodic visits by tiny cruise ships and infrequent cargo ships. But the benefits are great for those who make the trek—an unspoiled paradise is waiting for them.
- **2. Vulnerability to the Environment:**Overfishi

ng, climate change, and exotic species threaten Pitcairn's ecosystem's fragile balance. The island's distinct flora and wildlife, which have developed in isolation, are threatened by new species that could upset the natural balance. To lessen these risks and protect the biodiversity of the island, conservation initiatives are being carried out.

- **3. Self-sufficiency and Sustainability:**Pitcairn must be committed to sustainability and self-sufficiency because to its small population and scarce resources. The islanders depend on subsistence farming and fishing, and programmes supporting waste management and renewable energy sources are essential to the island's long-term survival. Pitcairn's natural beauty must always be preserved while still accommodating modern needs, which presents a constant challenge that calls for creative thinking.

- **4. Global Awareness and Cultural Preservation:**Another issue Pitcairn confronts is maintaining its distinct culture in the face of modern influences. Preserving the uniqueness of Pitcairn Islanders requires efforts to record and pass on their customs to future generations. At the same time, raising knowledge of Pitcairn's past, present, and attractions throughout the world is crucial to gaining support and admiration for this extraordinary region.

In summary

In summary, Pitcairn Island is a monument to the ways in which history, difficulties, and allure are intertwined. Its remoteness, historical importance, and distinct culture weave a tale that enthrals visitors who dare to explore its borders. Pitcairn allows the world to see its unique charm as it strikes a careful balance between progress and preservation. Pitcairn is a small island with a huge story, a microcosm of resiliency in the broad Pacific Ocean.

CHAPTER TWO

LOCATION AND GEOGRAPHY

A. LOCATIONAL COORDINATES

With accurate geographic coordinates, the mysterious treasure Pitcairn Island, hidden in the immensity of the South Pacific, reveals its mysteries. Located roughly at 25.07° S latitude and 130.10° W longitude, Pitcairn is one of the world's most isolated places. This puts it more than 3,000 miles (4,800 km) east of New Zealand, highlighting its remoteness and adding to the distinctive beauty of the island.

Pitcairn is a symbol of the majesty of the Pacific and the ability of life to persevere in the face of isolation. It is a member of the Pitcairn Islands group, which also consists of the Ducie, Henderson, and Oeno Islands. Pitcairn's location on Earth may be found via its geographic coordinates, which also provide doors to a world where nature, culture, and history all come together to tell an engrossing story.

B. THE ADJACENT WATERS

Pitcairn's charms reach far beyond its borders into the blue embrace of the neighboring Pacific Ocean. The identity of the island is greatly shaped by these seas, which are rich with mysteries from the past and aquatic life.

- **1.The Enormous Pacific Ocean :**Rising out of the expanse of the South Pacific, Pitcairn Island is encircled by a sea that reaches the horizon. Pitcairn is cradled in the vastness of the Pacific

Ocean, the largest and deepest ocean on Earth, which has moulded the island's ecosystems and affected its marine history.

- **2. Diversity of Marine Life:**Pitcairn's surrounding seas are well known for their transparency, which attracts divers and other marine enthusiasts with their glimpse of a world beneath the surface. Vibrant coral reefs, schools of tropical fish, and the magnificent presence of migrating species are just a few examples of the aquatic richness that surrounds the island.
- **3. Dynamics of Archipelagos:**The companions of the Pitcairn Islands group, the Ducie, Henderson, and Oeno Islands, make create a dispersed archipelago that enriches the surrounding waters. The

Pitcairn Islands are a sanctuary for scientists and environmentalists because of their diverse topography and marine environments, which weave together to form a tapestry of biodiversity.

- **4. Maritime Historical Significance:**The stories of the HMS Bounty and the mutiny that resulted in the founding of the island reverberate through the waters surrounding Pitcairn. Beneath the surface, the remains of the Bounty serve as a mute reminder of the historical events that took place in these marine stretches.

C. WEATHER AND CLIMATE PATTERNS

Pitcairn Island's temperature and weather patterns are shaped by its position in the Pacific Ocean and its geographic coordinates, which also provide a dynamic environment that supports life on the island.

- **1. Climate of Subtropicism:**Pitcairn has a subtropical climate with regular trade breezes and comfortable temperatures. Extreme heat is uncommon due to the moderating effect of the nearby water, making the environment suitable for both locals and guests.
- **2. Winds of Trade:**Originating from the subtropical high-pressure region, Pitcairn experiences refreshing breezes from the southeast trade winds, which also contribute to the weather's stability. The climate and vegetation of the island are significantly shaped by these trade winds.
- **3. Changes with the Seasons:**There are different wet and dry seasons in Pitcairn. There is more rainfall during the rainy season, which runs from November to March, and less precipitation

during the dry season, which runs from April to October. The island's landscapes are impacted by these cyclical changes, which encourage luxuriant flora during the rainy Season.

- **4. Variations in Climate:**Like many other Pacific islands, Pitcairn is vulnerable to abnormalities in the climate, with El Niño occurrences playing a major role. Variations in temperature, precipitation, and oceanic conditions can result from these anomalies. The ecosystems of the island exhibit a resilience that is indicative of the adaptation of life in this isolated region of the earth.

- **5. Effect on Day-to-Day Life:**The weather in Pitcairn has a profound impact on the daily life of the islanders. A vital component of water supply is rainwater collection, which replenishes reservoirs throughout the rainy season. Seasonal fluctuations also impact subsistence farming and fishing, underscoring the dependence on the natural environment.

In summary

In summary, Pitcairn Island's climate, surrounding waterways, and geographic coordinates combine to create a rich tapestry that defines the island's identity. Pitcairn's seclusion, highlighted by its exact coordinates, situates it in a world where the embrace of the Pacific Ocean defines its existence. The surrounding waters, rich in historical relics and marine life, add to the island's appeal as a biodiversity preserve.

The climate, which is shaped by trade winds and subtropical conditions, produces a relaxed yet lively atmosphere. The complex interrelationship between Pitcairn's residents and the natural environment is highlighted by seasonal fluctuations, climatic anomalies, and the influence on day-to-day living.

When we piece together Pitcairn's geographical journey, we find that it's more than just a dot on a map. We discover a world where human tenacity, environment, and history all come together, allowing us to recognise the connections between geography, culture, and the features that make this isolated Pacific paradise.

CHAPTER THREE

THE HISTORY AND HERITAGE

A. BOUNTY REBELLION AND AGREEMENT

Pitcairn Island's history is replete with drama and defiance, starting with the notorious HMS Bounty mutiny. Under Captain William Bligh's leadership, the Bounty sailed to Tahiti in 1789 in pursuit of breadfruit bushes.

But when dissatisfaction among the crew, spearheaded by Fletcher Christian, resulted in a mutiny against Bligh, the mission took an unfortunate turn.

- **1. A Mutiny Occurs:**On April 28, 1789, Fletcher Christian and a few other irate sailors took over the Bounty, sparking the start of the mutiny. The mutineers sought safety and secrecy with Tahitian acquaintances, while Captain Bligh and a few loyalists were abandoned on a small boat.
- **2. Pitcairn's discovery:**Fearing retaliation from the British Navy, Fletcher Christian and the other rebels looked for a secret haven. They found Pitcairn Island in 1790, an isolated island in the Pacific that appeared to have been abandoned. To evade discovery, the Bounty was scuttled, and the escapees,

accompanied by their Tahitian allies, created a covert community on Pitcairn.

- **3. Unsettling Starts:**Clashes with the Tahitian companions, internal strife, and survival challenges characterised the early years in Pitcairn. However, as European and Polynesian cultures mingled over time, a distinct society developed.

B. PITCAIRN IN THE PRESENT

Lineage and Traditions
This isolated island is still home to Pitcairn Islanders, the descendants of the Bounty mutineers. The way this little community has adapted and persevered throughout the years is demonstrated by its culture.

- **1. Demographics and Progeny:**There are about fifty people living in Pitcairn, a close-knit group of descendants who can trace their lineage back to the mutineers and

their Tahitian
companions. The island's
social structure is heavily
reliant on family
relationships, and the
descendants proudly
uphold the history of their
ancestors.

- **2. Vernacular and
  Customs:**Pitcairn's
  language is a variation of
  18th-century English
  mixed with Polynesian
  terms and idioms,
  demonstrating the distinct
  blending of cultures.
  Customs and festivities
  that are part of the
  island's cultural heritage,
  including Bounty Day,
  combine Polynesian
  influence with the island's
  maritime past.
- **3. Association with the
  Sea:**One distinctive
  feature of Pitcairn culture
  is still its relationship to
  the water. The customs of
  fishing, boat construction,
  and seafaring are carried
  down through the
  generations, representing

the island's survival and resiliency since its colonisation.

C. MAINTAINING HISTORIC SITES

In order to guarantee that Pitcairn's distinctive legacy is preserved for future generations, everyone works together to preserve the material artefacts from the island's past. A dedication to honouring the past and presenting it to the world is shown in the preservation of historical landmarks.

- **1. Bounty's Termination:**A moving reminder of what happened on Pitcairn is the mutineers' landing spot, often called Bounty's End. This historically significant location, which has been meticulously conserved, marks the initial landing spot of the Tahitian companions and the crew of the Bounty on the island.
- **2. The Grave of Fletcher Christian:**Another

significant historical location is the tomb of the mutineers' leader, Fletcher Christian. Nestled amidst the island's scenery, this tomb serves as a site of contemplation and respect, representing the multifaceted heritage of the man who was instrumental in Pitcairn's past.

- **3. Adamstown:**Pitcairn's lone settlement, Adamstown, is a living reminder of the island's past. Pitcairn's character is defined by its blend of European and Polynesian influences in its architecture, which is evident in both public and residential buildings.
- **4. The Anchor of Bounty:**An artefact that connects the island's maritime past and present is the anchor of the Bounty, which was discovered from the

waters surrounding Pitcairn. It is on exhibit and preserved, providing a physical link to the events of 1789 and the settlement that followed on Pitcairn.

- **5. Preservation and Record-Keeping:**In addition to the physical preservation of historical sites, ongoing conservation efforts also include recording oral histories and cultural practises. There are measures in place to protect the intangible cultural heritage of the island so that the legends surrounding Pitcairn live on beyond the tangible artefacts of the past.

In summary

In summary, the history and legacy of Pitcairn Island are braided together with strands of resiliency, rebellion, and cultural fusion. The narrative of Pitcairn Island is one of survival, adaptability, and the maintenance of a distinct cultural identity, spanning from the dramatic events of the Bounty mutiny to the island's current residents.

The dedication to maintaining historical sites is evidence of the islanders' understanding of the value of their cultural legacy. The stories of Pitcairn's past resound through its present, inviting the world to discover and enjoy this secluded Pacific gem as it continues to manage the difficulties of isolation and environmental sustainability. Pitcairn is a live example of the continuing force of human history and heritage because of the descendants of the Bounty mutineers, the subtle language variations, and the physical vestiges of history that stand as guardians of a legacy that transcends time and location.

CHAPTER FOUR

FLORA AND FAUNA

A. PITCAIRN'S BIODIVERSITY

Tucked away in the great South Pacific, Pitcairn Island is a biodiverse paradise where several ecosystems have developed on their own. The variety of the island demonstrates the tenacity of life in one of the world's most isolated regions.

- **1. Separation and Development:**Because of Pitcairn's remote location—more than 3,000 miles east of New Zealand—different ecosystems have been able to flourish. The emergence of rare plants and animals that are unique to Earth has been aided by the absence of natural predators and the minimal impact of Humans.
- **2. Varying Ecosystems:**Pitcairn has a variety of environments despite its tiny size, ranging from pristine beaches to rocky cliffs and verdant valleys. Numerous life forms

coexist in each microenvironment, resulting in a mosaic of biodiversity that enthrals both scientists and nature lovers.

- **3. Wealth from the Sea:**The wildlife of Pitcairn's surrounding waterways is likewise abundant. A vast array of marine life, ranging from vibrant reef fish to magnificent pelagic species, can be found on coral reefs, seamounts, and underwater caverns. The island's reputation as a worldwide hotspot for biodiversity is largely due to its maritime environments.

B. DISTINCTIVE ANIMAL AND PLANT SPECIES

- **1. Plants:**Pitcairnia feliciana: A unique native to Pitcairn, this bromeliad plant is distinguished by its vivid red flower and rosette of green leaves. Found in the island's highland forests, it represents the distinct flora that has developed independently.

Henderson Island Mallow (Kokia hendersoniana): Located on Pitcairn, this endangered plant is named for the adjoining Henderson Island. It symbolises the connectivity of the Pitcairn Islands' flora with its hibiscus-like flowers.

- **2. Animal Life:**The native Pitcairn Reed Warbler (Acrocephalus vaughani) is a representative of the island's rich bird life. The Pitcairn Reed Warbler, with its lovely song and unique patterns, is a symbol of the natural diversity of the island.

Pitcairn Islands Booby (Sula sula): This seabird species has a distinctive feeding habit and is found on Pitcairn and nearby islands. Its remarkable look and adaptations to marine life highlight how crucial the surrounding ocean is to the biodiversity of Pitcairn.

C. PRESERVATION INITIATIVES

The people who live on Pitcairn Island have taken on the role of custodians of this natural gem, working together with global conservation groups to maintain and safeguard the island's distinctive flora and fauna.

- **1. Areas of Marine Protection (MPA):**Pitcairn has created one of the world's largest marine protected areas after realising the importance of the nearby waterways. Covering an area of 834,334 square kilometres, the MPA promotes the preservation of marine biodiversity by protecting important habitats such as seamounts and underwater ecosystems.
- **2. Management of Invasive Species:**Pitcairn's ecosystems are threatened by invading species, both plant and animal. Programmes for

managing invasive species are part of conservation efforts, with the goal of controlling and eliminating non-native species that could upset the delicate balance of the island's biodiversity.

- **3. Preservation of Endemic Species:**Initiatives for conservation give special consideration to endemic plant and animal species. Conservationists may design strategies to preserve and improve the habitats of these species by comprehending the distinct ecological niches they occupy. This will help to ensure the long-term survival of Pitcairn's rare riches.

- **4. Ecological Methods:**In order to reduce their environmental impact, the people of Pitcairn Island actively participate in sustainable practises. These initiatives, which range from waste management to ethical fishing methods, seek to reconcile the demands of ecological conservation with human needs

- **5. Research in Science:**To comprehend and protect Pitcairn's biodiversity, ongoing scientific research is essential. Research collaborations between domestic and foreign scientists broaden our awareness of distant island ecosystems globally and add to the body of knowledge, which in turn informs conservation policies.

In summary

In summary, Pitcairn Island is revealed to be a biodiversity hotspot worthy of preservation and appreciation in addition to a historical and cultural asset. Centuries of seclusion have sculpted the island's distinctive flora and wildlife, creating a delicate tapestry that represents the island's biological resiliency.

Pitcairn Islanders are committed to maintaining the island's biodiversity, as seen by their conservation initiatives, which are supported by the international community. These initiatives—which range from the creation of marine protected areas to the control of invasive species and sustainable practices—serve as a paradigm for striking a balance between the necessity of protecting the natural world and human existence.

Pitcairn's biodiversity serves as a lighthouse, reminding us of the interconnection of all species on Earth as it navigates the challenges of the contemporary period. The history and legacy of the island are not limited to human history; it is also a story of coexistence with nature, one that encourages people to take responsibility for safeguarding and appreciating the natural treasures that enhance our planet.

CHAPTER FIVE

TRAVEL TO PITCAIRN

A: EASILY REACHABLE

Pitcairn Island has a unique difficulty and attraction in terms of accessibility because of its isolated location in the huge South Pacific. Travellers' sense of adventure and maritime exploration have defined the trip to this remote sanctuary, making it an experience in and of itself.

- **1. Isolation and Seclusion :**Due to its remote location—more than 3,000 miles east of New Zealand—Pitcairn must be reached by a lengthy maritime journey. Restricted accessibility has served as a barrier as well as a safeguard, keeping the island's unspoiled natural surroundings and distinctive cultural legacy intact.

- **2. A Sea Journey:**The main way to get to Pitcairn is by boat; the island is only seldom serviced by cargo ships. These ships, which frequently leave from New Zealand, are a lifeline for transportation and supplies, but due to weather and logistical issues, their itineraries can be erratic.

- **3. Restricted Air Travel:**Pitcairn does not have a dedicated airport, in contrast to certain other isolated islands. Although there have been talks of possible air access, building a runway would be difficult due to the island's tiny size and rough terrain. The main way to get to Pitcairn is still by boat as of right now.

- **4. An Exciting Journey for the Brave Traveller:**Not for the timid, the journey to Pitcairn draws adventurers and those looking for an experience away from the typical route. For those who embark on the journey, the prospect of reaching one of the most isolated inhabited locations on Earth lends an air of exclusivity and thrill.

B. GREEN TOURISM APPROACHES

Pitcairn Island adopts a commitment to sustainable tourist practises despite its restricted accessibility. The inhabitants of the island understand the fine line that must be drawn between welcoming tourists into their home and protecting the natural and cultural integrity of this special place.

- 1. **Minimal Impact of Visitors:**Pitcairn's yearly tourist count is small, which helps to minimise its environmental impact. By ensuring that the influx of tourists does not impair the pure quality of the landscapes, this deliberate approach to tourism helps conserve the island's delicate ecosystems.

- **2. Interaction of Cultures:**Residents of Pitcairn Island proactively share aspects of their culture with guests, providing an insight into their way of life. Respectful interactions are a top priority for sustainable tourism practises, which also promote awareness of the island's history, customs, and difficulties of living in such remote isolation.

- **3. Conscientious Exploration:**Pitcairn guided tours and excursions follow responsible exploring guidelines. There are rules in place to minimise disturbances to the island's wildlife and plant life, and visitors are educated about the vulnerability of the ecosystems. Maintaining Pitcairn's attraction as a tourist destination requires utmost respect for the natural environment.

- **4. Participation in the Community:**The people of Pitcairn take an active involvement in tourism-related projects by providing lodging, regional goods, and guided tours. In addition to supporting the island's economic viability, this involvement makes inhabitants and visitors feel more accountable for protecting Pitcairn's distinctive character.

C. THEMES FOR TOURIST INTEREST

Accessibility may be a problem, but adventurous visitors will find a wealth of fascinating sites on Pitcairn Island. A tapestry of activities that satiate the adventurous soul may be found on the island, ranging from historical landmarks to spectacular natural beauties.

- **1. Bounty's Termination:**The mutineers' landing spot, Bounty's End, is historically significant and a good place for tourists interested in learning more about the island's past to begin their exploration. This historical landmark provides a setting against which the story of the mutiny and the remains of the Bounty come to life.
- **2. The Cave of Christian:**The leader of the Bounty mutineers, Fletcher Christian, is connected to a naturally occurring cave in Pitcairn. In addition to offering a breathtaking viewpoint, Christian's Cave makes a concrete link to the difficulties the mutineers encountered in the early years of settlement.
- **3. Adamstown:**The lone village on Pitcairn,

Adamstown, is a quaint community that offers a window into islanders' daily lives. Explore the distinctive architecture of the area, engage with the locals, and become fully immersed in the culture that has developed over many generations.

- **4. Wonders of the Marine World:**For dive lovers, the oceanic environment surrounding Pitcairn is a veritable gold mine. Divers will find fascinating dive locations with their diverse marine life, underground caverns, and pristine coral reefs. By supporting the well-being of these ecosystems, the marine protected area gives tourists access to a vibrant and sustainable undersea experience.
- **5. Day Trip to Henderson Island:**Boats may take you to Henderson Island, which is a part of the Pitcairn Islands group and

a UNESCO World Heritage Site. Visitors can see this unspoiled atoll, which is home to rare plant and bird species, on a day excursion to Henderson. Travelling there gives you the opportunity to see the Pitcairn Islands' diversity from outside the main town.

- **6. Stargazing:**Pitcairn is an excellent location for stargazing because it is free of light pollution. Marvel at the celestial wonders of the Southern Hemisphere, such as the Milky Way and constellations that are difficult to see in more populated locations.

In summary

In summary, Pitcairn Island tourism is a careful balancing act between sustainability, accessibility, and the wonders in store for daring travellers. Due to its restricted accessibility, the island attracts visitors looking for an uncommon and off-the-beaten-path excursion, adding to its exclusivity.

Pitcairn's sustainable tourism practises demonstrate the island's dedication to protecting its natural and cultural assets. Intentional low impact, cross-cultural interactions, responsible exploration, and community involvement all help to create a tourist paradigm that honours the precarious equilibrium between human interaction and environmental preservation.

Pitcairn provides a rich tapestry of attractions for travellers, ranging from historical landmarks and natural beauty to engaging cultural experiences. The island's stories—of rebellion, resiliency, and the peaceful coexistence of a small society with the expanse of the South Pacific—are just as captivating as its beautiful landscapes.

CHAPTER SIX

LOCAL LIFE AND CULTURE

A. COMMUNITY AND POPULATION

Tucked away in the warm embrace of the broad South Pacific, Pitcairn Island is more than just a place; it's a vibrant community with a diverse range of local customs and ways of life. The people who live in Pitcairn are descended from the Bounty mutineers and their Tahitian allies, and they are the essence of this special island.

- **1. Close-knit Community:**Pitcairn has a small population of about fifty people living there. The close-knit relationships, familial ties, and communal spirit that characterise this small village define day-to-day life on the island. The small population encourages a sense of community and shared accountability.

- **2. A Legacy Across Generations:**Pitcairn Islanders have a multigenerational legacy that dates back to the Bounty mutiny events. The island's character is still being shaped by the descendants of the mutineers and their Tahitian partners, who make sure that historical motifs are ingrained in daily life.
- **3. Cooperative Living:**Pitcairn's remoteness has led to the emergence of a distinctive community lifestyle. Islanders share resources and responsibilities in a way that goes beyond conventional community structures, depending on one another for assistance. The pleasures and difficulties of living on a secluded island foster a strong sense of

41

camaraderie among the populace.

- **4. A Lifestyle of Subsistence:**Pitcairn's subsistence way of life is centred on farming, fishing, and group endeavours. Islanders depend on sustainable practises to meet their everyday requirements since they have a close relationship with the land and the water. This way of life not only keeps the community going, but it also cultivates a great regard for the environment.

B. CUSTOMS AND HOLIDAYS

The customs and celebrations that make up Pitcairn Island's cultural fabric are woven with the tenacity, past, and colourful legacy of its people. These generations-old customs are more than merely occasions; they are dynamic representations of Pitcairn's distinct culture.

- **1. National Bounty Day:**Celebrated on January 23rd, Bounty Day is a significant event in Pitcairn's cultural calendar. This celebration honours the Bounty mutineers' entrance on the island in 1790. On this day, people reenact, dance, share meals, and contemplate the history of the island's origin.
- **2. Customary Motions:**An important part of Pitcairn's cultural expression is through traditional dances. These dances, which have European and Polynesian influences, are a live link to the island's past rather than merely performances. Islanders use vibrant clothing and rhythmic gestures to display their own blend of cultures.
- **3. Dialect:**The dialect used in Pitcairn is a unique form of English from the eighteenth

century, enhanced by vocabulary and idioms from Polynesia. This language blending is evidence of the blending of cultures that took place when the island was settled. The language serves as more than just a tool for communication; it is a living legacy that ties the neighbourhood to its history.

- **4. Art and Handicrafts:**Islanders create things that highlight their ingenuity and cultural history through traditional handicrafts and art forms. Crafts like weaving and wood carving are creative manifestations of the customs and narratives that have been passed down through the ages, not merely useful abilities.
- **5. Religious Ceremonies:**A major part of Pitcairn's social and cultural life is the church. Sunday church

services are social events where locals congregate to worship, exchange news, and deepen their sense of community in addition to being religious celebrations. The church acts as a hub for social and spiritual interactions.

- **6. Easter Holidays:**On Pitcairn, Easter is a special time of year marked by church celebrations and neighbourhood activities. To celebrate the resurrection of Christ, islanders get together and combine customs with social events and shared feasts. The islanders' feeling of togetherness and faith are reflected in Easter.
- **7. Cultural Interaction with Guests:**An essential component of Pitcairn's traditions is the sharing of cultures with tourists. The people of the island extend a warm welcome to visitors,

sharing their traditions, legends, and way of life. In addition to presenting tourists to Pitcairn's culture, this exchange gives the locals a chance to interact with and learn from the global community.

C. REGIONAL FOOD AND SAVOURY TREATS

The cuisine of Pitcairn Island is a reflection of the island's distinct past, its natural resources, and the ingenuity of its people. The remoteness of the island has influenced its food, which now depends on the abundance of the nearby sea and the lush soil to create mouthwatering dishes that are a tale of creativity and survival.

- **1. The Seafood Festival:**Because Pitcairn is so close to the Pacific Ocean, fish plays a major role in the native diet. There are many different ways to prepare fresh catches, such as fish, lobster, and crab, ranging from grilling to cooking techniques used in traditional Pacific island cuisine. The island's dependence on the water for nourishment is evident in its seafood offerings.

- **2. Tropical Fruits and Root Vegetables:**Tropical fruits and root vegetables can be grown on Pitcairn's lush land. Bananas, sweet potatoes, yams, and taro are main foods in the area. These ingredients add to the gastronomic diversity of the island in addition to being nutrient-dense.

- **3. Conventional Cooking Methods:**Cooking methods that have been passed down through the years are used by islanders. Earth ovens are a traditional method used for special events, where food is wrapped in leaves and cooked slowly in pits. The community maintains a link to its Polynesian heritage through this age-old custom.

- **4. Creative Coconuts:**A common ingredient in many Pitcairn recipes, coconuts are abundant throughout the Pacific. A popular ingredient that gives richness and flavour to both savoury and sweet dishes is coconut cream. Cooks on the islands demonstrate their inventiveness by using coconuts in a variety of dishes.
- **5. Social Feasts:**Pitcairn's culinary culture is vibrantly expressed through community feasts. These get-togethers, which are frequently connected to festivals and special events, include a variety of foods made by various community members. Gatherings for communal feasts honour food and the island's overall spirit.
- **6. Original Modifications:**Pitcairn's

seclusion has inspired inventive culinary modifications. Islanders produce dishes that showcase their resourcefulness in the culinary arts by utilising creative ways and locally sourced materials. This flexibility is evidence of the community's capacity to flourish in a demanding setting.

- **7. Heritage in Culinary Arts:**Recipes and cooking customs are passed down, preserving Pitcairn's culinary legacy. Every meal narrates the history of the island, the blending of various cultural influences, and the customs of everyday communal life. Cooking legacy is a celebration of identity and common experiences, not merely a means of subsistence.

D. MAINTAINING CUSTOMS IN A CHANGING ENVIRONMENT

The preservation of local life, cultural customs, and culinary history becomes a dynamic process of adaptation and conservation as Pitcairn Island navigates the challenges of the modern period. The islanders understand how important it is to connect with the larger global community while yet embracing their own identity.

- **1. Instruction in Culture:**Tradition preservation is greatly aided by cultural education. Younger generations receive active instruction from islanders in language, dances, handicrafts, and culinary customs. The preservation and growth of Pitcairn's cultural heritage is guaranteed by cultural education.
- **2. Worldwide Networking:**Technology has made it easier for Pitcairn to be connected globally. The islanders communicate their stories, customs, and

cultural practises with the
world through the
internet and other
communication
technology, despite their
physical isolation. This
international involvement
offers a forum for
intercultural dialogue and
understanding.

- **3. Eco-Friendly
  Methods:**Sustainability
  encompasses Pitcairn's
  cultural customs.
  Islanders are aware of the
  importance of
  maintaining their customs
  in a way that respects the
  environment.
  Sustainability is a guiding
  concept in both cultural
  and environmental
  endeavours, whether it is
  through the use of locally
  obtained ingredients, eco-
  friendly handicrafts, or
  sustainable fishing
  techniques.
- **4. Participation in the
  Community:**Maintainin
  g the vitality of Pitcairn's
  traditions requires active

community participation in cultural preservation initiatives. Residents can actively contribute to the preservation of their cultural heritage through community activities, workshops, and cooperative initiatives, which promotes a sense of shared responsibility.

- **5. Making Adjustments:**People from Pitcairn Islands have a unique capacity for changing adaptation without sacrificing their essential character. Pitcairn's traditions are robust and relevant because of the community's capacity to adapt, whether it's through creative means of preserving their culinary heritage or the incorporation of new aspects into traditional festivities.

In summary
In summary, despite its remote location, Pitcairn Island is a

tribute to the tenacity of the
native way of life, cultural
customs, and delectable cuisine.
The small community spins a
story that ties together the past,
present, and future. It is firmly
anchored in its
multigenerational tradition.
Customs and celebrations are
more than just shows; they are
dynamic manifestations of
Pitcairn's distinct character. The
island's cultural fabric is a
colourful representation of its
history, sense of community,
and blending of many
influences, from Bounty Day
celebrations to traditional
dances.
Pitcairn's culinary delights
weave a tale of tenacity,
inventiveness, and
resourcefulness. The island's
food is a celebration of regional
ingredients and the capacity for
creativity and adaptation among
the people, enhanced by the
bounty of the sea and the
fertility of the land.
The dynamic process of
conservation and adaptation
that is the preservation of local

life, cultural traditions, and culinary history continues as Pitcairn Island navigates the currents of change. With their strong ties to both the land and the water, the islanders continue to tell a tale that touches people all over the world—that of a strong community that perseveres in the face of the difficulties and beauty of the South Pacific.

CHAPTER SEVEN

OBSERVATION AND

PRESERVATION

A. ENVIRONMENTAL ISSUES

Pitcairn Island has a variety of environmental issues that need for cautious attention and conservation efforts due to its remote position and delicate ecosystems. The residents of Pitcairn Island face difficulties that necessitate a balanced coexistence between human survival and the preservation of the island's natural treasures as stewards of this Pacific gem.

- **1. Impact of Climate Change:**For Pitcairn, the effects of climate change are a major worry. The biodiversity of the island and its coastal habitats are in danger due to rising sea levels, shifting weather patterns, and ocean acidification. Because of the island's susceptibility to these climate-related changes, protective measures for its natural resources are needed.

- **2. Non-native Animals:**Pitcairn's distinctive ecosystems are seriously threatened by invasive species of both plants and animals. Native plants and animals may be outcompeted by non-native species, upsetting the delicate equilibrium that has developed over many years. In order to protect the biodiversity of the island, conservation efforts involve the management and eradication of invasive species.

- **3. Waste Management and Limited Resources**:There are issues because the island has little facilities for garbage handling and land. It is imperative to implement sustainable waste management practises in order to avert environmental damage and safeguard the island's unspoiled features. Pitcairn faces a challenging problem in reconciling the need for resources with environmental sustainability.

B. INITIATIVES FOR SUSTAINABLE DEVELOPMENT

People who live on Pitcairn Island understand how important it is to undertake sustainable development projects that both solve environmental issues and promote community well-being. Through these measures, the island's natural and cultural history will be preserved while also taking social dynamics and economic requirements into consideration.

- **1. Areas of Marine Protection (MPA):**The creation of a Marine Protected Area (MPA) is one of Pitcairn's historic sustainable development projects. With its 834,334 square kilometres, the MPA is among the world's largest. In addition to encouraging the sustainable use of marine resources, this conservation policy attempts to safeguard important marine environments, such as seamounts and distinctive underwater ecosystems.
- **2. Sources of Renewable Energy:**Pitcairn's commitment to sustainable development includes embracing

renewable energy sources. In particular, solar power contributes significantly to lessening the island's need on conventional energy sources. The use of renewable energy is consistent with international initiatives to reduce climate change's effects and advance environmental sustainability.

- **3. Eco-Friendly Fishing Methods:**Pitcairn's way of life revolves around fishing, and the island's future depends on sustainable fishing methods. The community emphasises the value of protecting fish populations and sustaining the wellbeing of marine ecosystems by using ethical fishing techniques. This strategy makes sure that fishing is a viable source of income for those living in Pitcairn Islands.

- **4. Innovation in Agriculture:**One of the most important components of sustainable development in Pitcairn is agricultural innovation. Because of the island's small land area, creative methods are needed to maintain the ecosystem while maximising agricultural yield. Methods like organic farming and permaculture help ensure sustainable land usage and food production.
- **5. Ecotourism Projects:**Pitcairn has welcomed eco-tourism efforts in recognition of the possible effects of tourism on the ecosystem. The goal of these projects is to minimise the environmental impact while offering tourists engaging and one-of-a-kind experiences. The tourism industry in Pitcairn is more sustainable when it

include guided tours,
educational initiatives,
and ethical travel
practises.

C. JUGGLING TOURISM AND PRESERVATION

The increasing number of
tourists visiting Pitcairn
presents a dilemma in
maintaining the island's
unspoiled ecosystems while still
catering to the needs of the
tourism industry. It takes careful
planning, community
involvement, and a dedication to
ethical tourist practises to strike
this delicate balance.

- **1. Restricted Accessibility as a Factor in Preservation:**Pitcairn's restricted accessibility has served as a natural preservation to some degree. The number of visitors has been hampered by the island's remote position and difficult access. Because of its exclusivity, Pitcairn's natural ecosystems and cultural legacy have been preserved.

- **2. Conscientious Travel Approaches:**Residents of Pitcairn Island actively promote ethical travel practises. Tourists receive education regarding cultural sensitivities, the vulnerability of the island's ecosystems, and the significance of reducing their influence. The goal of polite encounters and guided tours is to make sure that tourism helps the island achieve its conservation objectives.
- **3. Development of Sustainable Infrastructure:**The development of tourism infrastructure is guided by the notion of sustainability. The goal of managing and designing accommodations, facilities, and transportation is to have the least negative

influence on the environment. The overall objective of striking a balance between tourism and the preservation of Pitcairn's distinctive identity is in line with the incorporation of sustainable infrastructure.

- **4. Tourism and Community Involvement:**The people of Pitcairn take an active part in tourist efforts and reap the rewards. The community's economy is bolstered by locally owned lodging, islanders leading excursions, and the selling of handcrafted goods. Incorporating locals within the tourism sector guarantees that the sector reflects the goals and values of the community.
- **5. Regulation and Surveillance:**Maintaining a balance between tourism and preservation requires a strong monitoring and regulatory framework. Visitor

activities are subject to stringent standards and regulations in order to protect cultural sites and delicate ecosystems. Adaptive management is made possible by continuous monitoring, which guarantees that the influence of tourism stays within sustainable bounds.Cooperative Preservation: A Joint Obligation

In summary, Pitcairn Island confronts environmental issues that call for coordinated and ongoing conservation efforts. The islanders are actively involved in protecting their natural and cultural heritage, which includes tackling invasive species, supporting sustainable development, and reducing the effects of climate change. Initiatives for sustainable development, such as the creation of a sizable Marine Protected Area and the use of renewable energy, demonstrate Pitcairn's dedication to a future that coexists peacefully with its distinctive ecosystems. The careful balancing act between environmental conservation and economic growth is evidence of the island's commitment to long-term sustainability. Pitcairn takes great care in navigating the delicate issue of balancing tourism and preservation. Sustainable infrastructure development, community involvement, and responsible tourism practises all contribute to a strategy that values tourism while preserving the island's unique identity. In the face of the intricate relationship between conservation and problems, Pitcairn's residents are unwavering in their resolve to take care of their precious Pacific treasure. Pitcairn's story is about more than simply isolation and resiliency—it's about a community that accepts its duty to protect its place of origin for future generations. Pitcairn Island welcomes everyone to join in the conservation journey, which is resonant with the echoes of its

past and the promise of a
sustainable future, via
cooperation, ingenuity, and a
shared sense of purpose.

CHAPTER EIGHT

CHALLENGES AND
MAINTENANCE

A. CONCERNS ABOUT THE
ENVIRONMENT

Pitcairn Island's remote location
and fragile ecosystems make it a
target for conservation
initiatives and careful attention
to a range of environmental
challenges. As guardians of this
Pacific gem, the people who live
on Pitcairn Island must balance
human survival with the
preservation of the island's
natural resources.

- **1. The effects of
  climate change:**The
  implications of climate
  change are a big concern
  for Pitcairn. Ocean
  acidification, changing
  weather patterns, and

increasing sea levels are putting the island's biodiversity and its coastal habitats under jeopardy. The island's natural resources require protection because of its vulnerability to these climate-related changes.

- **2. Exotic Animals:**Invasive plant and animal species pose a severe danger to Pitcairn's unique ecosystems. The delicate balance that has established over many years may be disturbed if non-native species outcompete local flora and animals. Management and eradication of invasive species are key components of conservation efforts aimed at safeguarding the island's biodiversity.

- **3. Resource constraints and waste management:**There are problems because the island doesn't have enough area or infrastructure for disposing of waste. Using sustainable waste management techniques is essential to preventing environmental harm and preserving the island's natural features. Pitcairn has a difficult time balancing resource needs with environmental sustainability

B. SUSTAINABLE DEVELOPMENT INITIATIVES

Residents of Pitcairn Island are aware of the significance of pursuing sustainable development initiatives that address environmental problems and advance the welfare of the local population. By taking these steps, social dynamics and economic needs will be taken into account while simultaneously protecting the island's natural and cultural legacy.

- **1. Marine Protection Areas (MPA):**One of the iconic sustainable development initiatives of

Pitcairn is the establishment of a Marine Protected Area (MPA). Situated on 834,334 square kilometres, the MPA is one of the biggest in the world. This conservation policy aims to protect significant marine environments like seamounts and unique underwater ecosystems, while also promoting the sustainable use of marine resources.

2. Renewable Energy Sources:
One aspect of Pitcairn's commitment to sustainable development is the use of renewable energy. Specifically, solar energy plays a major role in reducing the island's reliance on traditional energy sources. Utilising renewable energy aligns with global endeavours to mitigate the impacts of climate change and promote environmental sustainability.

3. Sustainable Fishing Techniques:
Fishing is the main industry in Pitcairn, and using sustainable

fishing techniques is essential to the island's survival. By employing ethical fishing methods, the group highlights the need of maintaining fish populations and the health of marine ecosystems. This plan ensures that the people who live in the Pitcairn Islands can make a life from fishing.

4. Agricultural Innovation: Innovation in agriculture is one of the keystones of Pitcairn's sustainable development. The island's restricted land area means that innovative techniques are required to maximise agricultural productivity while preserving the ecosystem. Techniques like permaculture and organic farming contribute to the sustainable use of land and production of food.

5. Projects related to ecotourism:
Given that tourism may have an impact on the environment, Pitcairn has embraced eco-tourism initiatives. These initiatives aim to provide tourists with unique and

engaging experiences while minimising their negative effects on the environment. When it comes to ethical travel practises, educational programmes, and guided tours, Pitcairn's tourist sector is more sustainable.

C. Handshaking Travel and Conservation

Maintaining Pitcairn's pristine ecosystems while also meeting the demands of the tourism sector is made more difficult by the growing number of visitors. To achieve this delicate balance, community involvement, careful planning, and a commitment to ethical tourism practises are necessary.

1. Limited Accessibility as a Preservation Factor:

Pitcairn's inaccessible location has partially acted as a natural preservation. This secluded location and challenging access to the island have limited the number of visitors. Pitcairn's natural ecosystems and cultural heritage have survived because of its exclusivity.

2. Travelling with conscience:

Pitcairn Islanders aggressively encourage moral travel behaviour. Visitors are taught about cultural sensitivity, the island's ecosystems' fragility, and the importance of lessening their impact. Encouraging interactions and tour guides aim to ensure that tourism contributes to the island's conservation efforts.

3. Creating Sustainable Infrastructure:

The concept of sustainability directs the construction of tourism infrastructure. Managing and planning transportation, lodging, and facilities with the least amount of adverse environmental impact is the aim. The integration of sustainable infrastructure aligns with the overarching goal of finding a balance between tourism and the preservation of Pitcairn's unique identity.

4. Tourism and Involvement in Community:

The residents of Pitcairn actively participate in tourism initiatives and profit from it. Locally owned hotels, islanders leading tours, and the sale of homemade handicrafts all contribute to the community's economy. Locals' aspirations and values are guaranteed to be reflected in the tourism sector when they are involved.

5. Control and Monitoring: Striving for equilibrium between tourism and preservation necessitates a robust regulatory and oversight structure. Strict guidelines and rules apply to visitor activities to safeguard sensitive ecosystems and cultural places. Continuous monitoring ensures that the impact of tourism stays within sustainable bounds, enabling adaptive management.Collaborative Preservation: A Shared Responsibility

In conclusion, Pitcairn Island faces environmental challenges that necessitate concerted and continuous conservation efforts. The islanders aggressively combat invasive species, promote sustainable development, and lessen the consequences of climate change in order to preserve their natural and cultural heritage. Sustainable development initiatives, like the establishment of a large Marine Protected Area and the use of renewable energy, show Pitcairn's commitment to a future in which its unique ecosystems coexist harmoniously. The meticulous equilibrium struck between preservation of the environment and economic expansion is proof of the island's dedication to enduring sustainability.

Pitcairn navigates the tricky business of striking a balance between tourism and preservation with remarkable care. Responsible tourist practises, community involvement, and sustainable infrastructure development all support an island-wide tourism policy that values visitors while maintaining its distinct character.

The people of Pitcairn remain adamant in their desire to protect their priceless Pacific treasure, despite the complex interplay that exists between conservation and challenges. The tale of Pitcairn is about a community that recognises its responsibility to preserve its place of origin for future generations; it is about more than just isolation and perseverance. With collaboration, creativity, and a common goal, Pitcairn Island invites everyone to partake in the conservation journey that is resonant with the echoes of its past and the promise of a sustainable future.

CHAPTER NINE

PRACTICAL INFORMATION FOR TRAVELERS

A. TRAVEL ARRANGEMENTS

- **1. Arriving:**Although it is difficult to get to Pitcairn Island, one of the most isolated inhabited places on Earth, the trek is surely worthwhile for those looking for a distinctive and off-the-beaten-path experience. The main means of transportation on the island is the water because there are no airports. The MV Claymore II is the sole regular passenger ship that sails from Mangareva, French Polynesia, to Pitcairn. Tahiti is the starting point for flights to Mangareva. Due to the wide seas, travellers should be aware that the journey to Pitcairn can be difficult. It is imperative to verify the most recent details and make reservations well in advance as the MV Claymore II runs on a seasonal basis and schedules are subject to alteration. It takes about 32 hours to complete the trip, so travellers should be ready for motion sickness.

- **2. Conditions for Entrance:**Before visiting Pitcairn, visitors must receive authorization from the Pitcairn Island Council. This entails filling out an application and giving information on the visit's goals, itinerary, and lodging arrangements. In addition, a valid passport is required for entry, and purchasing travel insurance is strongly advised.

Strict biosecurity guidelines are in place at Pitcairn to safeguard its distinctive ecosystem. Food, plants, and outdoor equipment are among the things that must be disclosed and inspected when carried onto the island. This keeps the delicate environmental balance of the island intact by preventing the entrance of unwanted species.

- **3. Money and Interaction:Pi**tcairn's official currency is the New Zealand Dollar (NZD). Although credit cards are accepted, it's best to have cash on hand for smaller purchases.

Visitors should make appropriate plans as there is no ATM on the island and only spotty internet and cell phone connection. Pitcairn's local time is in the same time zone as New Zealand.

B. LODGING AND AMENITIES

- **1. Motels:**Pitcairn's small population is reflected in the restricted number of accommodations available. Guesthouses and private rooms are available, giving guests a chance to experience the friendly hospitality of the neighbourhood. It is advised to reserve lodging well in advance, particularly during the busiest travel times, which fall between November and March, when temperatures are at their highest.

Travellers often choose the Bounty Homestead because it provides cosy accommodations with breathtaking views of the island. McCoy's Lodge is an additional choice that is renowned for its warm ambiance and attentive service. These lodging options offer a special opportunity to engage with the amiable inhabitants and fully immerse oneself in the island's culture.

- **2. Facilities and Services:** Despite being a far-off location, Pitcairn provides all the necessities for travellers to have a comfortable stay. There's a general store on the island where you may buy snacks, necessities, and mementos. For individuals who are interested in the history and culture of the island, the Pitcairn Island Study Centre is an invaluable resource.

Although medical services are offered, it is recommended that guests pack any essential prescriptions and speak with a healthcare provider before departing. A church, a post office, and a small school on the island offer a glimpse into Pitcairner daily life. It is important for visitors to keep in mind that the island is a cash economy, meaning that access to some products and services could be restricted.

C. A GUIDE TO CONSCIENTIOUS TRAVEL

- **1. Preservation of the Environment:**Pitcairn Island is home to a diverse range of plants and animals, and it has an immaculate natural setting. To protect the fragile ecosystem, tourism must be conducted responsibly. It is important for visitors to follow the biosecurity guidelines and refrain from bringing non-native species into the island. There are hiking trails available, but in order to reduce your influence on the surrounding flora and fauna, you must stick to the authorised paths.

Travellers can experience the island's natural beauty while leaving as little of an environmental impact as possible by taking part in organised eco-friendly tours. Participating in conservation-related activities, such as beach clean-ups and informative tours provided by neighbourhood environmental organisations, is urged of responsible tourists.

- **2. Sensitivity to Culture:**It is imperative to show respect for the customs and culture of the locals when visiting Pitcairn. The people on the island are friendly and welcoming, and the community is close-knit. In order to respect people's privacy, you must obtain permission before taking any pictures of them or their property. The sustainable growth of the island is facilitated by taking part in local activities and buying handcrafted items from local craftsmen.

It's recommended that visitors educate themselves about Pitcairn's history and legacy; guided excursions can offer valuable insights into the island's past. Aware of the small population and scarce resources, guests should make an effort to reduce trash and preserve water while visiting.

- **3. Involvement in the Community:**Getting to know the locals is one of the most rewarding experiences of a trip to Pitcairn. To feel the welcoming mood, go to community events like Sunday church services or island get-togethers. Talking with the inhabitants helps one have a better grasp of their way of life and the difficulties they encounter.

Additionally, there can be volunteer options that let visitors make a beneficial impact on the community while they're there. Participating in cultural events or helping with environmental conservation projects are two examples of experiences that create a lasting impression on both locals and tourists by fostering a sense of community.

In summary

For those who are ready to go off the usual road, Pitcairn Island provides an incredible vacation experience with its distant appeal and distinctive cultural heritage. Careful planning is necessary for the logistics of travel, and responsible tourism is essential to protecting the island's natural beauty and bolstering its tight-knit population. Through a spirit of adventure and consideration for the fragile nature and culture of Pitcairn, travellers may create a journey that is both genuinely unforgettable and helps to support the growth of this far-off paradise.

CHAPTER TEN

PITCAIRN ISLAND'S FUTURE

Pitcairn Island is an isolated refuge of resilience, and its future remains a question mark as it stands at the crossroads of its past and contemporary concerns. The island's future is deeply entwined with its efforts to save the environment, preserve its cultural legacy, and strike a careful balance between sustainable growth and its allure.

- **1. Care of the Environment:**A key component of Pitcairn Island's future is its dedication to environmental conservation. The Marine Protected Area (MPA) and programmes for renewable energy and sustainable fishing practises demonstrate the island's commitment to protecting its natural resources. Navigating the effects of climate change, guarding against alien species, and making sure Pitcairn's ecosystems stay strong and biodiverse are the continuous challenges.

- **2. Ecological Advancement:**The future of Pitcairn depends on how carefully economic growth and environmental sustainability are balanced. Eco-tourism and innovative agriculture are just two examples of sustainable projects that are crucial to ensuring the island's economic prosperity in the future without sacrificing its distinctive ecosystems. Because of the island's tiny population, careful planning is required to create a harmonic balance between development and preservation.

- **3. Legacy of Culture:**Pitcairn's multigenerational settlers' legacy is a live example of the island's diverse cultural heritage. Pitcairn's future is in the hands of its people, who take an active role in both cultural adaptation and preservation. In order to preserve Pitcairn's distinct identity over time, it is crucial that newer generations be taught about the island's cultural traditions while it navigates these shifting currents.
- **4. Conscientious Travel:**Responsible travel is the cornerstone of Pitcairn's tourism industry. The island's natural buffer of restricted accessibility offers a chance to sculpt tourism in a sustainable way. Promoting conscientious behaviour, including the community, and having a profound understanding

of the island's vulnerability will be essential to guaranteeing that tourism plays a constructive role in Pitcairn's future.

- **5. Cooperative Preservation:**The future of Pitcairn is inextricably linked to cooperative conservation initiatives. The preservation of the island's distinctive ecosystems depends on continued research, assistance from international efforts, and the active participation of the local people. Pitcairn's problems are not unique; they are a reflection of the larger global conversation about protecting isolated and delicate ecosystems.

B. PROMOTING APPRECIATION AND PRESERVATION

- **1. Awareness of the world:**Increasing international awareness is the first step towards promoting Pitcairn Island preservation and appreciation. Pitcairn's distinct attractiveness stems from its distant location, rich wildlife, and rich cultural legacy. To protect the island's future, recognition and assistance from other countries are essential. Documentaries, educational initiatives, and outreach campaigns can all be effective means of fostering a sense of worldwide respect and accountability for Pitcairn.

- **2. Instruction and Cross-Cultural Communication:**In order to promote respect for Pitcairn's natural and cultural resources, education is essential. Collaborative educational initiatives can foster cultural interaction, environmental awareness, and a greater comprehension of Pitcairn's struggles and achievements both locally

and internationally.
Pitcairn can encourage a
sense of custodianship
among a variety of
audiences by telling its
narrative.

- 3. **Long-Term
  Collaborations:**Creatin
  g long-lasting alliances is
  crucial to Pitcairn's long-
  term sustainability.
  Working together with
  scholarly institutions,
  international conservation
  organisations, and ethical
  travel companies can
  benefit the island by
  providing resources,
  experience, and a
  common goal. Pitcairn has
  the opportunity to
  improve its standing
  internationally by
  collaborating with
  organisations that share
  its commitment to
  conservation and cultural
  preservation.
- 4. **Empowerment of
  the
  Community:**Appreciatio
  n and preservation are

intrinsically related to local community empowerment. A sense of pride and ownership is fostered by encouraging locals to actively participate in conservation efforts, offering economic possibilities, and supporting local projects. The community's impact is extensive and long-lasting when its members are committed to the preservation of their house.

- **5. Honoring Achievements:**Emphasising achievements is a potent technique to promote appreciation and preservation. These tales are sources of inspiration, whether they deal with the effective preservation of a rare species, the adoption of sustainable methods, or the resuscitation of cultural customs. By recognising successes, Pitcairn can inspire others to support the preservation of the island by demonstrating the beneficial results of teamwork.

C. CONCLUDING REMARKS ON PITCAIRN'S PARTICULAR ALLURE

As the story of Pitcairn Island comes to an end, it is impossible to not be struck by the island's singular charm—a tapestry woven with strands of solitude, resiliency, and the unwavering spirit of its people. Pitcairn is more than just a place; it's a dynamic example of how adaptable people can be, how they can conserve the environment, and how they can preserve cultural history.

- **1. The Seduction of Seclusion:**Pitcairn's seclusion, which used to be a source of misery, is now one of its main attractions. Because of its isolation, the island is a virgin wilderness where nature can flourish unhindered by modern influences. Pitcairn presents a unique chance for the daring traveller to enter a realm where history reverberates in the sea breeze and time appears to have stopped.

- **2. Adaptability in the Face of Adversity:**Pitcairn's tale is one of resiliency, handed down through the years by islanders who overcame adversity with courage and tenacity. Pitcairn Islanders, through the Bounty Mutiny and the complexity of today's environmental concerns, have persevered through rough seas with unwavering devotion to their homeland. The island's tenacity serves as a contemporary example of the people's unwavering spirit rather than merely being a historical footnote.
- **3. Using conservation as a compass:**Pitcairn's distinctive charm is

inextricably linked to its dedication to conservation. Sustainable fishing methods, the establishment of the Marine Protected Area, and environmental awareness campaigns highlight the island's commitment to protecting its natural treasures. Pitcairn's position as a protector of its ecosystems adds to its appeal as a travel destination that supports sustainability in a world when unspoiled habitats are becoming fewer and further between.

- **4. The Living Legacy of Cultural Heritage:**Pitcairn's appeal is further enhanced by the legacy of its cultural heritage that is still alive today. For those who come, the customs, language, and tales that have been passed down through the ages weave a singular tapestry.

Pitcairn's rich cultural legacy is not a thing of the past; rather, it is a dynamic statement of identity that invites guests to join in on the story as it unfolds.

- **5. An Appeal for Conscientious Exploration:**Pitcairn's distinct attraction extends a call for responsible exploration, to people who want adventure but also a closer relationship with the places they go through. The visitor's experience becomes infused with collaborative conservation, responsible tourism, and a dedication to preservation. Pitcairn invites travellers to walk carefully, feel deeply, and add significantly to the continuing tale of this amazing island.

Every thread in the tale of Pitcairn symbolises a turning point, an obstacle overcome, and a victory acknowledged. Pitcairn Island's distinct charm is becoming a beacon for the future, guiding people towards responsible stewardship, worldwide appreciation, and the lasting legacy of a place where culture and nature blend into an extraordinary dance that calls on everyone to join in maintaining Pitcairn Island's magic.

Printed in Great Britain
by Amazon

40548486R00056